Stay Safe on Wet Days

By Cameron Macintosh

It is wet and grey
outside today!

It is raining,
and the wind is wailing.

These trees sway in the wind.
They bend with the strain!

We must try to stay safe on days like this.

Branches may break
and fall from trees,
so it is best to stay inside.

“Play inside today,” said Dad.

“Yes, there is no way I will play outside!” said Faith.

There is so much rain!

It is so wet that the drains cannot take in all the rain.

This lady got stuck in the rain.
She had to wait for aid.

It has been frosty
where Shay lives.

Shay made this trail
in the thick white slush
as she walked.

Shay's dad put chains on the van.

The chains weigh a lot, but they help the van to not slip.

Today, there is a lot of slush on the main street.

Look where you step!
You may slip and fall.

The best way is to walk
like a snail!

Shay has a great time on a sleigh.

Frosty days are not so bad!

CHECKING FOR MEANING

1. Why is it safer inside than outside on very windy days? *(Literal)*
2. What might happen if people are not careful when walking on icy or frosty paths? *(Literal)*
3. What does it mean to *walk like a snail*? *(Inferential)*

EXTENDING VOCABULARY

wailing	What is the base of the word *wailing*? What does wailing sound like? What else can wail, besides the wind?
aid	What does the word *aid* mean? What is another word the author could have used instead of *aid*?
main	Which letters in the word *main* make the long /ā/ sound? What makes a street the main street of a town? How is it different from other streets?

MOVING BEYOND THE TEXT

1. What are some things you can do inside when the weather is rainy or windy?
2. Do you enjoy wet weather? Why?
3. What kind of clothes should you wear on a rainy day?
4. Why is rain important? How might it help a garden?

TIME TO WRITE

Write about your favourite thing to do on rainy days.

PRACTICE WORDS

main
snail
great
raining
grey
today
sleigh
stay
may
they
play
aid
wailing
lady
break
drains
chains
days
weigh
rain
Shay
Faith
way
wait
trail
strain
Shay's
sway